# Angels
## Everywhere

ANGELS EVERYWHERE by Lynn Valentine

Published by PREMIUM PRESS AMERICA

ISBN 1-887654-76-3

Library of Congress Catalog Card Number 99-74535

PREMIUM PRESS AMERICA gift books are available at special discounts for premiums, sales promotions, fund-raising, or educational use. For details contact the Publisher at P.O. Box 159015, Nashville, TN 37215, or phone toll free (800) 891-7323 or (615)256-8484, or fax us at (615)256-8624.

For more information visit our web site at *www.premiumpress.com.*

Editor Mardy Fones
Cover and Interior Design by Bob Bubnis/BookSetters—bksetters@aol.com
Printed by Vaughan Printing

First Edition 1999
1 2 3 4 5 6 7 8 9 10

# Angels Everywhere

Miracles

&

Messages

## Lynn Valentine

PREMIUM PRESS AMERICA
NASHVILLE, TENNESSEE

**an·gel n.** An immortal being attendant upon God; a very kind and lovable person; a helping or guiding spirit.

# Table of Contents

## *Introduction*

> *Do not forget to entertain strangers,*
> *for by so doing some people have*
> *entertained angels without knowing it.*
> —Hebrews 13:2 NIV

It's funny how you can go to church for years and years and never quite get it. Maybe you are like I was not all that long ago, where part of you believes and part of you wonders.

When I started this book, I did so planning to take it on more like a journalist studying the phenomena of Angel sightings. I dug into everything I could find — the Bible, books by Bible scholars, obscure books, out-of-print books, articles and even the Internet to learn as much as I could about these heavenly beings.

It wasn't until I began reading and interviewing those who claimed to have had encounters with Angels, that this book took on a new meaning for me. Suddenly, in that place where heart, intellect and spirit all meet, I knew that it was real.

It is my prayer that regardless of what you believe about Angels, that you will be inspired and turn the last page with a renewed hope. I know I have.

Yours Very Truly,

Lynn Valentine

# Dedication

To God.

I'm no poet and I can hardly call myself a writer after the book you've written. But this work is dedicated to you. I pray you are thinking . . . "Well done, my good and faithful servant."

The angel of the Lord encamps around those who honor Him … and He delivers them.

—Psalm 34:8

# Acknowledgement

In compiling this book and interviewing the witnesses to these events I was moved time and time again by the desire of these people to share their stories with the world. The stories that they regarded as private, personal and too fantastic to share became a testimony to them and almost the fulfillment of a life purpose to share these words and experiences with you.

As I talked with these people, friendships were born which I will take with me forever. I would like to acknowledge now the special contribution of the following people ...

# Angels Everywhere

Maddy — Thanks for always re-charging my batteries with your enthusiasm.

Shirley—Thanks for helping me wrap this up in such a mighty way.

Andie — A friend and a poet. A diamond in the rough.

Sharon — Thank you for opening up your heart to share.

Deborah —Thank you for not leaving out the best part.

Chris — Thanks for all the giggling. I sure needed that.

Donna — I will never be able to look at a butterfly the same again. (HUG)

George and Bette — Thanks for believing in me . . . AGAIN!

Thank you to my family for patiently waiting for mommy to finish.

Thank you, Mom, I do BELIEVE.

And special thanks to all of those who submitted their stories to share. Your selfless acts of kindness to be of help and encouragement take my breath away. God Bless You.

To my husband, Bob, the unsung HERO in my life.

# "Be Calm"

On Jan. 17, 1994, a powerful earthquake jolted California. The magnitude 6.7 earthquake hit at 4:31 a.m. and caused severe damage throughout several communities, leaving many dead, hundreds of others injured and millions more frightened. The rumble was so loud in my townhouse I couldn't hear the walls around me cracking or the plates and windows breaking and shattering.

Anyone who has ever been through a big quake will relate to the helpless feeling you have afterward. The feeling of not being able to trust the ground you are standing on is undescribable. After the initial shock and seeing the extensive damage all around me, I had to get used to the constant aftershocks. Going upstairs to my bedroom terrified me. I, like many others, slept in my clothes with the lights on.

In mid-March 1994, we went through a particularly violent aftershock sequence. We had seven strong aftershocks all before daylight.

During one of these, I was holding on to the headboard of my bed, terrified as the bed violently shook. Suddenly, through the roar of the earthquake, I heard a Booming Voice saying, "Be Calm." The Voice was so loud it seemed the entire world should have heard it. It was a deep authoritative voice but unlike any voice I had ever heard. It was coming from the corner of my room, near a bookcase.

Upon hearing the Voice, I immediately felt a sense of peace. I grabbed a piece of paper and wrote down the words, "Be Calm." I placed the paper in a frame and put it inside the nightstand next to my bed.

The next day, I called my Mother to tell her about the voice. She thought it must have been an Angel or the Voice of God.

# Be Calm

The peace and serenity I felt stayed with me throughout other aftershocks. My friends in Los Angeles knew I was afraid of earthquakes, so they would call me right after the strong aftershocks to see if I was okay Each time they noticed I was calm and several of them asked me why I was no longer so fearful. I told them about the Booming Voice saying, "Be Calm."

In April of 1997, I was planning to drive 225 miles North to Fresno for my uncle's 90th birthday party. The trip involved driving through the Tehachapi mountains and the Grapevine, an earthquake-prone region. I kept telling myself I'd have no problem driving through this mountain pass, unless there was an earthquake.

Around 4:45 a.m. on the day of my planned trip, we had another strong earthquake and the epicenter was in the exact area I had to drive through.

Even though the epicenter was about 45 miles from my home, it was felt quite strongly throughout the Los Angeles area, stirring up the old fears.

# Angels Everywhere

As the ground was still shaking, I reached to turn the light on. I opened the night stand to get my flashlight in case the electricity went out but as I did, the framed "Be Calm" note I had written in the middle of the night three years earlier fell out and landed on the floor. My eyes fell upon those comforting words and I knew that my seeing them was no coincidence.

Reassured, that God and His Angels were protecting me, I packed my car and drove to Fresno for my uncle's birthday party. Driving right over the epicenter of the quake that had just struck two hours before, I felt a sense of peace and tranquillity. I quit looking down at the earth and began looking up into the sky and the beautiful mountains that lay before me.

I no longer leave the framed "Be Calm" message inside my nightstand. It sits on top of it where I can see it daily.

—*Kathy Fjermedal*
*Santa Monica, California*

# Just Passing Through

The winter of 1994 had been unforgettable due to the vast amounts of snowfall and ice that had crippled our area for weeks. However, the beginning of March had given us promise of nicer weather as Spring slowly inched its way around the corner, and Winter's worst temper tantrums had gradually ceased leaving only cold mornings, frost and ice blanketing the vulnerable outdoors.

As a schoolteacher, I left early each morning for my 20-minute drive to school. My youngest son, Joshua, would accompany me since he attended the same school. This time to and from school became a time of bonding throughout the years leaving precious memories.

The summer before, we had purchased a van; however, because of its extended top, we could not park it in our garage. On bitterly cold mornings, thick frost would form on my windows, forcing us to scrape them.

One morning as I was trying to scrape off a heavy coating of ice, my husband appeared in the driveway with a kettle of hot, steaming water and threw it on the front window of the van.

As my wipers raced back and forth, the ice did magically vanish, but within seconds, ice crystallized once again across my windshield leaving me frustrated. My husband became perturbed. He yelled for me to shut off the wipers, since he assumed they had caused the frost to reappear. He then got more hot water, and again, the ice miraculously melted.

"Don't turn your wipers on!" he ordered before going back inside. So, slowly down the driveway Josh and I ventured that dark, shivering cold morning. As I carefully crept out onto our street that led to the highway, a glaze of ice began to dance across my windshield; nevertheless, I still could slightly manage to see the road.

Realizing my windshield was crystallizing, Josh asked if I could see. I replied "barely" and with the defrosters still on high, I switched on my wipers hoping the ice would dissipate faster. By then, I had slowly driven out onto the highway. In horror, the condition worsened within seconds. The crystals became a thick opaque coat of milky white ice. Josh, this time screamed, "Mom, can you see?" A no nervously groaned from my lips. Except for a tiny peephole at the bottom of the windshield where the wipers had rested seconds ago, I was blind.

I began to tremble knowing full well we were headed for trouble and that I must pull off the highway; however, I could not see the road. My speed had diminished to a crawl. I was aware that I also could not see traffic behind me, around me or in front of me.

Suddenly, Josh yelled, "Mom, look at the light!"

I looked up from my peephole and saw through a glazed windshield a light so bright that it reminded me of train lights.

Shaking, I screamed out to Josh, "My God, he's on our side of the highway!"

"No, Mom, I think you are on his side!" he blurted out in terror.

The white line I had thought was the edge of the road was really the dividing line. Aloud, I pleaded with God and my guardian Angel to help me NOW! A blaring horn intensified my fear. I knew if I were in the wrong lane and pulled to the right, I might end up in the path of a car. I only had a fraction of a second to make my choice. Slowly, hoping any cars in that lane would allow me in, I eased my van to the right.

My body stiffened as I whispered, "Spare my son, God; please spare my son!" At that moment, a gush of wind rocked the van. Pebbles pelted its side. The lights that were upon us were overwhelming in brightness. Although the windows were up, a gust of wind passed through our vehicle. As our tires finally left the pavement and rolled slowly onto the shoulder, my body loosened, muscles began to shake and tears of thankfulness rolled down my cold cheeks.

We were safe! I looked out to see what I had just missed only to see the black of the night staring me in the face.

# Just Passing Through

To the passenger side of our van came a pounding and a familiar voice.

"Shirley, Shirley, are you all right?" My neighbor, Gail, had pulled in behind me.

She said she was driving a few car lengths from me and had watched the nightmare unfold. She went on to tell me that the vehicle that was upon us was an 18 wheeler.

As she questioned why I had been on "his" side of the road, I pointed to my windshield and explained briefly my error. Realizing I was in no condition to drive, she instructed me to remain in my van, and she would return shortly with my husband.

Later that evening, Gail called me to discuss once more my near-death experience. At the end of our conversation, she explained that she had hesitated to call me; however, she wanted to relate to me what she had actually witnessed that I could not have because of the blinding ice.

"You didn't make it, Shirley. I saw everything clearly, since I was behind you. You didn't make it, girl," she kept insisting.

"I don't understand, Gail. I did make it. God must have heard my cry or my Guardian Angel lost a few feathers on this one," I tried to jest.

"No, Shirley," she said, "I distinctly saw the semi-truck going through the side of your van as you tried pulling off the road. I could hardly believe what I was seeing but I did see it. You didn't make it."

I was stunned and speechless as she spoke. I knew, too, that the good Lord did hear my soul cry out on that cold, dark morning and gave us another chance for life. Why? I don't know. I just know now beyond the shadow of doubt, that there is someone watching us.

For years I have believed in Guardian Angels. In fact, I named mine long ago, Constance, since he is constantly watching over me.

Thank you Constance, for allowing us to pass through!

—*Shirley Lakes*
*Shepherdsville, Kentucky*

# My Angel

When I was little, we lived in an old two-story farm house with a steep staircase. It a landing about half way up before it angled off and went the rest of the way to the second floor.

I was playing with my toys one afternoon but eventually became bored and decided to go see what my mother was doing. As I hurried down the stairs, I lost my footing and began to fall.

That's when I saw someone standing on the landing. He was big and powerful looking and his frame shimmered. Although I probably would scream now if it happened again,

I was not afraid at the time. Watching the light dance and swirl about him was comforting like the soothing glow of a fireplace.

I realized then I was seeing an Angel.

As I watched him, I suddenly realized that I was not falling but floating very slowly toward him. It was like I was moving in slow motion.

"Don't be afraid." he said, "everything is going to be okay."

I drifted downward, as if I were being carried, until finally my feet came softly to the floor.

After I touched down, I looked up and saw that the Angel had vanished.

I went to tell my mom. When I said I had fallen down the stairs, she was worried at first, but became perplexed when she saw I was fine.

"What happened?" she asked.

"My Angel helped me."

I told her the whole story but I don't think she believed me then.

# My Angel

Years later, my mom and I were talking about Angels, and I brought up the encounter I had as a child. This time my age and the clarity of my recollection convinced her that on that day, my Guardian Angel really had stepped in to save me from injury.

As we wondered what God might have been sparing me from, my brother Aaron jumped in to share his theory.

He thinks that because I am a dancer and I do routines with a Christian message, that I was caught so I could dance for God.

It makes me feel like dancing just thinking about that.

*—Sarah Loutner*
*Springfield, Tennessee*

He will give His angels charge of you, to guard you in all your ways.
—Psalm 91:11

# Angel on Flight 1641

Everything had happened so fast. The ad in the magazine detailing the weekend seminar in Sedona, Arizona. The call to my travel agent. Flight reservations to Phoenix. Car rental arrangements for the 120-mile drive. Motel accommodations. Getting time off work during our busiest season and finding I had enough money to afford this spur-of-the-moment trip. This was certainly out of character for me. I never did anything on the spur of the moment.

I detested the monotony of car trips. My immediate comfort zone never takes me more than 35 miles in any direction. But here I was, sitting in seat 25D on Northwest Flight #1641, waiting for take-off.

# Angels Everywhere

My thoughts were interrupted by a heated discussion in the seats next to me. The occupants, an elderly couple, were having a disagreement about seating. They wound up moving across the aisle to other seats, only to create more commotion when the rightful occupants of those seats showed up. One of the young men took the window seat in my row, leaving the seat between us vacant. I don't know where his companion ended up as my thoughts were now focusing on something altogether different.

Were the walls really closing in on me? Why was it so difficult to catch my breath? I felt like screaming but couldn't. My heart was beating so fast and loud I felt it would jump out of my chest at any moment! All I could think of was getting OFF THE PLANE — but my legs would not move — and the aisle was completely blocked by boarding passengers. What was I going to do? I just had to get off that plane.

I dug my fingernails into the armrests of my seat, as if this could somehow help me hold on to reality but it only served to magnify the horror. How could I have been so incredibly stupid as to forget my fear of flying?

# Angel on Flight 1641

The last time I'd flown — seven years ago on a non-stop from Honolulu — the plane had taken a sudden drop in altitude too terrifying for words.

Drinks, snacks, stewardesses and unbuckled passengers were sent flying.

Even though the pilot assured us it was "just a little bit of unexpected turbulence," I'd vowed never to fly again. But here I sat, trapped on a plane still sitting at the gate, scared witless.

My racing thoughts were interrupted by a calm voice asking if the seat next to me was taken. Without looking up, I nodded and mumbled something about my being a white-knuckle flyer.

The voice responded "I know," as baggage was being stowed in the overhead compartment. *Was it really that obvious?* I wondered.

As he seated himself I noticed we were both wearing pale purple shirts.

How synchronistic, I thought but said nothing as I was still very much absorbed by my fear-of-flying mode. The next thing I knew he was prying my nails away from the armrest and gently took my hand to rest it between his. Under other circumstances I would've protested this obvious infringement of my space — but somehow this was different.

At first his words seemed to be coming from somewhere far away, and I could barely make them out. But it didn't take me long to tune in to what he was telling me. He gave me a detailed rundown of what was going on in the cockpit, assured me of the safety of the plane, alluded to his innumerable trips on just this type of aircraft, explained each creak, bump, grind and shimmy the plane made — almost before it happened. I was still in no condition to respond verbally, so I just kept nodding, at once indicating I understood what he was saying as well as encouraging him to keep talking.

He ordered a glass of Chablis for each of us. I eagerly accepted and at last could feel myself relaxing. Once I got my wits about me, I noticed my rescuer was a very attractive man. He had a mischievous twinkle in his eye and the most sincere smile I'd ever seen. Soon we were talking a mile a minute about practically every subject under the sun. In

# Angel on Flight 1641

what seemed like no time at all, the pilot was giving us our landing instructions.

I thanked the helpful stranger for his kindness and as we parted in the terminal, we shared an embrace only friends of long-standing would find comfortable.

In a moment he was gone. Only then did it occur to me that I didn't even know his name. I returned to the plane and asked the stewardess what the name of the gentleman seated next to me was. She looked at her manifest and with a puzzled expression said, "But ma'am, there was no one seated next to you. The manifest shows that seat flew empty."

A chill ran down my spine, and I smiled knowingly. It didn't really matter if I didn't know his name. I'd seen *Highway to Heaven* and *Touched By An Angel* enough times to believe the TV characters just might have real-world counterparts. And besides, who else would know the intricacies of flying better than the Angel seated next to me on Northwest Flight #1641?

—*Ilsa Troge*
*Santa Rosa, California*

Angels are speaking to all of us—Some of us are only listening better.

—Anonymous

# His love For His Children

As a small child, I was sick in bed and felt like I was suffocating. I looked up and over to the head of my bed and saw a glowing figure sitting very close to me. Somehow, I knew that was my Guardian Angel! Later in life, my mother told me that I had been very ill with pneumonia, to the point I was given the last rites. Knowing that, I now believe that my Angel protected me from death.

When I was in my 30s, my husband became suddenly and seriously ill.

# Angels Everywhere

I was sitting alone in the hospital waiting room. I was feeling very downhearted and afraid I would be left a widow at this young age. I was trying to pray to God when an elderly lady sat right next to me. Because the room was basically empty, she could have had any chair she wanted.

I exchanged the basic pleasantries with her, but I really didn't feel like talking. She kept chatting and then, in the midst of our conversation, she suddenly locked eyes with me. I've never seen such blue eyes and she held me with them. It was like she was looking down into my soul. She said, "Everything will be all right — just let go and let God." She got up to leave and the next minute she just wasn't there at all.

My husband did recover and is still alive today.

This year, I became seriously ill with chest pains. During this time, I had to make a week-long business trip to Texas.

My husband was concerned about me being alone but I insisted I would be all right and went on ahead.

# His Love for His Children

The week passed relatively pain free, and I prepared to leave. I had to return the rental car, then take the shuttle to the main terminal to check my baggage. As I started to carry my luggage to the shuttle bus, I got very fatigued and felt twinges in my chest. The shuttle bus door opened and I saw that there were three very steep stairs up to the on-board luggage rack. I looked at those stairs and doubted I could lift my baggage up to the rack.

About that time, I heard a voice say, "Let me help you with that" and I turned to see a handsome young man dressed in a beautiful camel coat, white vest, camel scarf and brown pants. He had reddish hair and really looked great. I smiled at him and all of a sudden, my luggage was in the rack! Understand that he did NOT board the shuttle to place my luggage in the rack. I looked at the luggage and turned to thank him and could not see him anywhere. There were very few people in the area, and I couldn't figure out how he disappeared within a matter of seconds.

# Angels Everywhere

Shortly thereafter, I had open heart surgery because the main artery in my heart was blocked. The day before my operation, my doctor told me if I had exerted myself into a heart attack, I would have dropped dead. It was then I realized that the young man was not REALLY a man at all, but an Angel that God had sent to save my life.

—*Kathy Ozanne*
*Thornton, Colorado*

# Angel at the Beach

One very hot weekend I decided to take my two daughters to the beach to cool off. We were playing in the sand building sand castles and making memories, when all of a sudden, a huge wave came up, catching us by surprise and knocking us down. Before I could get to my feet, another wave, even larger than the first, crashed over us.

Frantically, I fought my way to my knees, while grabbing my 3 year old. I could see my 5 year old was trying to get back on her feet but she was scooped up by the water and pulled farther from me. I was able to grab the end of her hair but she must have swallowed some water because she had blacked out.

With my 3 year old in one arm, and my other hand tied up holding on to my other daughter, it was like one of those tug-of-war matches. With each surge of the tide, I was being pulled across the line.

Then out of nowhere came this boy. Even though my daughter was under the water and out of sight, he quickly found her. He looked to be around 10 years old but he grabbed her up with such calmness and confidence that I released her into his care and watched as he brought her quickly to shore.

I managed to get to my older daughter's side. In seconds, she began coughing up water and regained her consciousness. I had not yet caught my own breath as I began crying. I couldn't believe how short of a time it could take to lose a loved one.

What could have happened had the boy not come in time . . . *wait, where is the boy?*

# Angel at the Beach

He was gone. He didn't wait around to be thanked, he didn't wait for reward.

I looked for him and asked others if they had seen him but nobody knew what I was talking about. He disappeared — just like that. I did not think anything of it until I came home that night. As I was praying and thanking God, I realized that that was not a normal circumstance. That was as Angel.

—*Marfi Barnes*
*Long Beach, California*

If we ever wish to know angels for what they truly are ... perhaps it is we who must first learn to fly.

—-Anonymous

# An Angel Visit

My father died in January 1996, It was my first major experience with death. I grew up as the oldest of seven in what many would describe as a pretty familiar brood of Irish Catholics, post-WWII and in the 60s. While we were each loved as individuals, it was a common perception that I was a Dad's girl. Even well into adulthood, this perception continued.

After my Father's death, I had to return to the ordinary chores of life and the routine of my job. With my body on automatic and my mind in neutral I put one foot in front of the other and went through the motions.

# Angels Everywhere

One day, as I pushed the shopping cart through the aisles of my favorite food store, I was distracted from my thoughts by the sound of a whimpering child running toward me. I can still see her long curly red hair as she passed. I didn't stop her and quietly battled within.

The well-trained eldest daughter was triggered to reach out to comfort her. The woman in recovery knew she could not save every crying child. The whimpering 10-year-old would have to find comfort from another.

At the end of the next aisle, she reappeared. This time there was no battle within me.

"Honey, what's wrong? Are you lost? Hold on to my basket." I never did touch her or guide her hand, yet she stopped and took hold of the front of my shopping cart. I continued to ask, "Did you lose your Mommy?"

"No," she said, "I lost my Daddy."

I felt the hot coal hit my throat and I wanted to cry out, "I just lost my Daddy, too." I knew my role and I carried it out so well. "Come on, Honey, we'll go look for him."

# An Angel Visit

I can still hear myself offering assurances several times in our strolling, "Don't worry, Honey, he won't leave you here. He won't leave the store without you. He's right here somewhere. We'll find him."

As soon as I said that, she took off running. It was as if she had suddenly seen him and vanished around the corner.

I strolled passed the checkout lines, looking for them. Nothing.

Again, I walked through, searching for the bright red locks of hair. There were only six short lines

*How could they have disappeared so quickly?*

She was gone.

Some folks might disagree with me, and think I was making something out of nothing but I believe she was an Angel. Looking back, I believe that little girl was God's messenger sent to be with me, to move with me through another step of grief toward healing.

—*Madeline J. Hartwell*
*Hansen, Idaho*

Death is not a period, only a comma.

　　　—Sign outside a country church

# The Accident that Never Was

It was Christmas Eve and I was driving to a friend's house during the hectic Los Angeles rush hour. The night was pitch black and it was raining so hard that visibility was nil. The three lanes of traffic on congested La Cienega Boulevard were stopped for a red light and my tiny white sports car was the last in a very long line of vehicles. I was in the far left lane, wedged next to a 2-foot high cement island, casually looking through my rear view mirror at the reflection of the street lights and holiday decorations on the dark, shiny wet street behind me when I saw the three cars. There was one in each lane racing towards the stopped traffic, exceeding the speed where they could safely stop. The cars suddenly slammed on their brakes and started sliding and swerving all over the road.

I knew for certain that my car would be hit and having no way to escape it, murmured, "Please, God, help me" as I braced for the impact. I kept looking in the mirror and watching the cars approach. Unexpectedly, I felt a very gentle tap at the back of my car followed by a slight lifting sensation but did not see a car hit me. I then heard the crash of the cars slamming into each other. I waited a few moments for the dust to settle and then got out to see what had happened and give assistance if anyone needed help.

I was surprised to find my car sitting on the cement island. I had not felt enough of an impact to have moved that far, plus the car was exactly parallel to its original position, as if it had been lifted and moved three or four feet to the left then set gently down. It seemed slightly strange but at the time I really didn't give it much thought.

Fortunately, no one was physically hurt, however there was considerable damage to several of the stopped cars and the three cars that had hit them. What amazed me was that everyone wanted to know how I was and how much damage my car had suffered. I said I was fine and that nothing had happened to me or my car as I was not hit. With that statement, several people stared at me in disbelief, asking "What do you mean nothing happened to you? We saw your car fly through the air! You got hit harder than anyone else here!"

We then walked around my car and observed that there was not one scratch or mark on it. We also realized that the position of my car was against all possible laws of physics.

I was thankful that there were so many witnesses to this incident as it opened my eyes to the miracle that had just taken place. From my perspective nothing happened.

# Angels Everywhere

After they told me of their perspectives, I realized that someone had protected me by lifting my car out of harm's way. Although I did not see or hear anything, I know the gentle tap and lift that I felt had to have been from my Guardian Angel.

*—Troika Celeste Germain*
*Mount Shasta, California*

## WHISPER OF ANGEL WINGS

Today I stumbled and once again

Was lifted up by an unseen hand.

What comfort and joy that knowledge brings.

For I hear the whisper of angel wings.

The guardian angels God sends to all

To bear us up when we stumble and fall.

Trust Him, my friend, and often you'll hear

The whisper of angel wings hovering near.

—Author unknown

"There is rejoicing in the presence of the angels of God over one sinner who repents."

— Luke 15:10 NIV

# The Happiest Day

My mother was an invalid when she passed away. Her strength and vitality had been eroded by the passage of time but she had a strong spirit and that kind of strength that comes from a certain knowledge that life here on earth is nothing more than a prelude for what is ahead. Still though, despite her infirmities, her death was completely unexpected.

# Angels Everywhere

She seemed so alive to me, so it was difficult for me to be suddenly without her. To make matters worse, my brother was in the military and far away, leaving just me to deal with all of the details. In the midst of all of the funeral arrangements, I would cry out to God, asking Him for help — for strength and comfort and peace of mind. Still, I had no relief.

Even in the midst of my prayer time, I could not sense that He was anywhere close by. I basically felt alone.

I contacted my brother and planned the funeral for as late possible but it was doubtful he would make it.

Then came time to deal with choosing the music. Mom had told me weeks before she passed, that she wanted a particular song played at her funeral. It was called, "My God and I."

The music director agreed to sing it and the morning of the funeral, my brother did manage to get there. Still, even as the funeral was in progress, I was struggling with God and this feeling like he had not come through for me.

Then something marvelous happened. As the singer began to do the song, I began listening to the words and taking in the beauty of it all.

# The Happiest Day

I looked out over the markers and the neatly cut lawn to see something incredible.

There, off in the distance, I saw Mom. She was holding the hand of an Angel, and he was leading her away. Her legs were strong again — the infirmities were gone.

She did not look back at those of us who were left behind. I suppose she was far too excited about what lay ahead — after all, she was about to have the happiest day of her life.

*—Ruth Busby*
*Goodletsville, Tennessee*

How shall we tell an angel from another guest?
　　How, from the common worldly herd,
　　One of the blest?
Hint of suppressed Halo, Rustle of hidden wings,
　　wafture of heavenly frankincense which is
　　these things?
The old Sphinx smile so subtly: "I would warn the
　　world,
Treat well whom thou call'st fool."

— Gertrude Hall

# Stranded

I am a trucker and on one cold night after an ice storm in Lansing, Michigan I had an encounter with an Angel.

The roads were hazardous so I followed another truck on our way to make a grocery store warehouse delivery. I had only been there once before, so I was trying to keep up with him but somehow, I managed to lose him anyway.

I spotted our exit and got off the freeway but my partner was nowhere in sight. Thinking I had a pretty good idea of where I was going, I took a left but soon I was lost. Calling my partner on the CB radio, I learned that I had undershot the road I needed to take and had miles to go before I could get back on track.

Distressed, I began looking for a place to turn around but the streets just got darker and more ice covered as I went along. I found myself in an industrial area that hadn't seen an salt truck all night long. Finally, I came across an empty intersection that looked wide enough to get my big rig going the other way.

Wrong.

I was on solid ice and after several minutes of maneuvering, I ended up being stuck with no way to go backward or forward. I was alone and miles away from any help. Looking up I said, "God, you could really help me if you wanted to!"

No sooner than I uttered that prayer, a salt truck appeared out of nowhere. He salted the road all around me and even got out and gave hand signals to keep me out of the roadside ditch as I got back in the right direction.

I rounded the corner and was so happy to finally be back on my way. I pulled over to the side of the road to thank him.

# Stranded

The salt truck was gone.

Not so much as 15 seconds had elapsed since I saw him and I could easily see more than a half mile in every direction but he had vanished.

I initially thought it was odd that a salt truck would be out so far away from travelled streets but once it disappeared, I remembered my prayer to the Almighty and realized that I wasn't stranded after all.

—*Mike Harrington*
*Warrenville, Illinois*

I saw the tracks of angels in the earth. The beauty of heaven walking by itself on the world.

— Petrarch

# My One-eyed Angel

It was during the Christmas holidays, and my husband, two children and I went shopping in a larger city 100 miles away. There we met my sister and her husband. We had a lot of shopping and visiting ahead of us but were not in a hurry and planned to make a day of it. It was 11 p.m. when we finally started for home, tired but happy

We were still 36 miles from home when it began to snow quite furiously. The closer we got to home, the worse the roads were. The snow was coming down so hard we had trouble staying in our lane of the highway. My husband slowed to 10 miles an hour but still we had problems staying on the road. Unable to see the road and distinguish it from the ditches and canyons, I began to pray for God to send His Angels to help us. I picked up our cellular phone and called my sister. They had made it home to another town with no problems. I asked for them to pray for us. She and her husband immediately knelt and prayed for our safety.

By now my husband's eyes were tired of straining and we were weaving all over the road. It seemed we were the only ones on the road so late. Suddenly from a distance behind, I spotted a single headlight. It was coming at us at a remarkable speed considering the road conditions and heaviness of the snow falling. In a moment it was right behind us. I told my husband that someone else must be just as insane as we were. Then around us came the light.

Where it passed, it left a set of tire tracks, steady and true for us to follow. It travelled faster than what we could keep up and soon was out of sight. Still, even though snow was coming down heavily, the tires tracks left behind by the light remained free and clear. We followed them for several miles. The snow stopped falling so hard and we picked up speed.

Just as quickly as the headlight had appeared, the tracks suddenly ended. No turning, no exiting, no pulling off to the side, these tracks just ended as if the vehicle had lifted off the ground. I looked at my husband and told him I knew who was driving ahead of us. He looked at me in surprise and asked me who it was. I told him it was one of our Guardian Angels. He shook his head affirmatively as we pulled into our drive. We both thanked God for our safe arrival, and for giving us our Guardian Angels. Even if it's a one-eyed one.

—*Nola Jones*
*Fargo, North Dakota*

To love for the sake of being loved is human,
but to love for the sake of loving is angelic.

—Alphonse de Lamartine

# A Mothers Love

My mother had suffered from diabetes, kidney failure and finally cancer of the colon. She passed away with my two older brothers and myself by her bedside.

As she took her last breaths I thought to myself, *how could I go on without this wonderful lady who had nurtured me into the man that I had become?*

Approximately three months after we buried Mom I was looking through the window, feeling depressed. As I sat there, I drifted off to sleep and dreamed I was walking down this road. I looked to my left at a beautiful field and saw a large tree about 100 yards away. As I kept looking at this tree I saw a brilliant white light move from behind it. I was amazed at the brightness. I felt attracted to it and started walking toward it. It looked like a diamond reflecting the sun. When I got about 15 yards away, the light subsided and I saw my Mother's face. She had a white gown on and looked beautiful. Before she passed away, mom had one of her legs amputated from the diabetes but she had both legs now. She smiled and looked at me and held her arms out to hug me.

As she wrapped her arms around me, she said, "I love you and I know you love me but you have to go on with your life and be there for the people that depend on you. I have been preparing you for this all your life."

She also said that she was fine and that her father, sister and brother and others who preceded her in death were there taking good care of her.

She slowly moved backward looking so peaceful and serene, until the light again enveloped her. I watched the light until I could no longer see it. At the precise moment it

# A Mothers Love

disappeared I was awakened by a noise at the front door. I got up to see if someone there and found the screen door wide open. I immediately noticed there was no one around and that there was no wind at all to blow it open. I knew without a doubt that Mom was leaving and this was to show me that I wasn't dreaming.

—*Mike La Broi*
*Gary, Indiana*

In the arms of the Angel...

May you find, some comfort here.

—Sarah McLachlan
From her song "Angel"

# Are You Still Mad?

About a week after my son was killed in an accident, I decided to go to one of the Alcoholics Anonymous meetings he'd been attending. I planned to talk to them about drinking and driving. It seemed like the right thing to do. I had so much that I wanted to say . . . so much hurt to get out.

I said I was angry with God and that I had told God not to speak to me and that I would not speak to Him anymore.

I left the room not feeling any better and started back home.

# Angels Everywhere

I decided to go to the local K-Mart while I was out and cut over to a side street as a short cut.

It was a similar street to the one my boy was killed on.

As I drove, I thought about this and about the meeting. Suddenly, I looked up to see red flashing lights in front of me. I slammed on the brakes and skidded to a halt only about six feet from the semi-truck ahead of me.

A voice said to me, "This is what happened to your son. He did not see the truck. Are you still mad?"

I immediately pulled to the side of the road and apologized to God. I knew He had sent an Angel.

—*Donna Theisen*
*Fort Myers, Florida*

# GUARDIAN ANGEL PRAYER

Angel of God, my guardian dear,

To whom God's love commits me here.

Ever this day be at my side,

To light and guard to rule and guide

—Author unknown.

"The more materialistic science becomes, the more angels shall I paint: their wings are my protest in favor of the immortality of the soul."

—Sir Edward Coley Burne-Jones

# The Ushering

Stella Margaret Heck was a saintly woman. She was the daughter of a Methodist preacher, a firm believer and a true example of a Proverbs 31 woman. At 90 years old, she was a witness to everyone and as a grandmother, she was an especially inspiring person to me.

Tragically, she fell ill in the spring of 1985. There was nothing they could do for her but help manage her pain and wait.

The pain was great, too. Thankfully, she was unconscious most of the time but on those few occasions when she did awaken, her eyes told the story of suffering in ways that words could not fully describe.

# Angels Everywhere

On Easter Sunday, about 5 a.m., I was awakened by a breeze. It was more than a breeze really, growing to a wind. This wind was not coming from a window but rather from the wall behind my bed.

The wind grew in intensity and I became fully awake. I kept my eyes closed as I enjoyed the sensation of having this warm fragrant wind rushing over me. It was powerful but not violent. Strong and yet soft at the same time.

As I lay there, I can't say how I knew but I realized that something special was happening, something holy.

I opened my eyes and saw this light gold mist riding the wind. And then, in the midst of the wind, I was able to make out the barely visible, translucent outlines of huge powerful wings. They did not have feathers as you see in paintings but clearly, they were wings. They had a silver sheen to them with highlights of gold.

I knew right these were Angels, taking her to heaven.

—*Rebecca Brown*
*Springfield, Tennessee*

# *Kelly*

**K**elly, had just had her fourth birthday shortly before the car accident. She was everything to our family — the glue that had held us all together. We didn't know that until we lost her.

I had just dropped off my other two daughters at school and was on our way home when the car was broadsided by four cars. She wasn't wearing a seatbelt, (this was back in 1971 before it was law) and ended up with severe injuries.

She never woke up.

She was in St. Mary's Hospital in the ICU for eight days before the doctors unplugged the life supports.

# Angels Everywhere

One night, soon after, I woke up and saw a light in the doorway. Sitting up in bed, I saw Kelly standing there.

"Mommy, Don't be afraid." she said. "I'm all right."

My eyes filled with tears as the agony poured out.

"You can't come with me now. But, someday we'll be together again. Don't cry anymore, Mommy. I love you".

Kelly turned and vanished into the arms of waiting Angels.

—*Linda Darlene*
*South Gate, California*

*P.S. Always buckle up your children, and if you see some-one who forgets to do it, be a Guardian Angel and remind them.*

# An Angel with Robin's Wings

It was Christmas Eve of 1992 when my marriage began to come apart. I had known something was wrong for several months but when my husband failed to join the three kids and I for our traditional Christmas dinner at my parent's house I knew things were about to get bad. When we got back to our house that evening, Santa had been there but Daddy was not.

I cried my way through the night. I had never felt so depressed or so alone.

# Angels Everywhere

The next morning, my husband called to tell me he wanted a separation. He came, picked up his stuff and was gone. Days turned to weeks, weeks turned to months.

I work as a hairdresser and one evening, a customer who I had never seen before, walked right up to me and said, "Chris, can you fix my hair? Julie usually does it but she isn't here."

I was taken by surprise because I had no recollection of ever having met her or seen her at the shop before. She acted like a regular customer and yet I could not place her face.

She said her name was Robin and I went through Julie's customer card file so I could get an idea of what this customer usually had done. Despite the fact that Julie always kept her card file up to date, no card for Robin existed.

Making the best of it, I found out what she wanted and began working. Somehow though, as I fixed her hair, she began to extract from me the story of my broken marriage. I told her we would probably be getting a divorce soon.

# An Angel with Robin's Wings

As she looked at me it was like she was seeing straight into my heart. She began quoting scripture — one after the other, each one speaking to some aspect of my pain and suffering. I felt so much love and caring coming from her that I can't describe just how it felt. It was as if I were the most important person in the world to her.

I felt so much better as we spoke and was even a bit disappointed that I had finished her hair. As I began turning her chair so she could see how it came out, she stopped me to look in my eyes. "You will get back together and you'll have a great marriage . . . it will all work out!"

She stood up and said she didn't need to look in the mirror — she knew that her hair looked fine and left me with a smile. In all my years as a hairdresser, *that* had never happened before.

A few days later, I asked Julie about her. She had no idea who I was talking about and Robin never returned to the shop.

# Angels Everywhere

Early one morning, not long after that, I awoke to find my husband knocking at the door. He wanted to know if I would take him back. We talked and eventually worked things out. He and I are like two different people now and I can honestly say our marriage couldn't be better.

I believe that Robin was an Angel sent to lift me out of the lowest time of my life. To this day I never look at a Robin without smiling and wondering if she is just checking in on me.

*—Chris Steinke*
*Hastings, Michigan*

Every time you hear a bell ring, it means that some angel's just got his wings.

—Henry Travers to Jimmy Stewart in *It's A Wonderful Life*

"For He shall give his angels charge over thee to keep thee in all thy ways."

—Psalms 91:11

# Go to the Light

I had just arrived at my school around 7:30 a.m. when our school secretary paged me over the intercom for an important message. Had my husband locked himself out of the house again? Could a parent of one of my students be calling this early? These thoughts and more flooded my mind as I raced down each hall to the main office.

Upon entering, I realized something must be seriously wrong by the look on our secretary's face. I braced myself as she said without hesitating, "Go home, Shirley. Your father is dying." As my eyes teared and overflowed, I began to realize that the event that I had dreaded my whole lifetime was now becoming a reality.

My father had been 42 when my twin sister and I were born. At an early age, I increasingly became conscious that my dad appeared to always be the oldest father among parents who accompanied their children to school functions. Sometimes a few of my friends would question, "Is that your grandpa or dad?" Eventually, I became very alarmed about Dad's age; as I entered high school, apprehension about still having my father upon graduation clouded my thoughts. He would be almost 60! Now, as I looked back I realized my worrying was needless for I had not only graduated high school but had earned my master's degree 17 years prior. I had been given an abundance of treasured years with him.

With tears streaming down my face, my heart pounded nervously as I rushed home to gather my family and head off for my hometown and my father's side.

For years, I had dreamed of being the one to help him depart this world without fear for Dad had not been a Christian or spoken much of God until these last few years. Thankfully, little signs from him told me he had started a closer walk with Him.

In silence, my husband drove the three hours to Vincennes while I silently prayed for God to allow me to see and speak once more with my father before he died.

Since my father had wrestled with two previous bouts of pneumonia that year, his strength and resistance were low. Just the night before, I had chatted with him long distance after discovering he had returned to the hospital. He assured me there was nothing to worry about.

"Sissy, I'll still be here this weekend. You can come up then," was his soft reply. We talked and laughed for nearly an hour and I honestly felt that I would have that weekend to be near him once more.

As I dashed down the halls of the hospital to Intensive Care, my twin greeted me. She informed me of his perilous condition and how the doctors and staff had desperately worked trying to raise his blood pressure which had dangerously dropped. His condition quickly deteriorated.

# Angels Everywhere

Quietly entering his room, I could see life-support machines by his bed and a ventilator which prevented him from speaking. Though it allowed him to breathe, it painfully robbed him of his last words to me.

I sat tensely beside him taking his frail hand in mine, patting it and announcing that I was by his side now. I looked deep into his hazel eyes and knew the candle was burning out.

I talked to him for a brief time, just the two of us alone in the sanitized room of humming machines, the thread that allowed him to still be apart of this world. I knew God had generously allowed me this extra moment to talk to him. I gently kissed his cool brow and whispered, "Dad, do you know you're dying?"

Looking tenderly into my eyes and trying to smile, he nodded, yes and gazed at the foot of his bed. Trying to ease any fears he may have, I once more squeezed Dad's hand and whispered, "Dad, God is here and loves you. He will lead you over to the other side. Don't be afraid."

Excitedly, he tried to raise up and pointed adamantly to the foot of his bed. He tried to say something but the ventilator prevented him. "Dad, is someone here?" Repeatedly, he pointed to the foot of his bed and nodded, yes.

I began to tremble for I knew what would very soon take place. There were only two of us in that room; however, my Dad's three dimensions were now four.

I motioned for the nurse to hurry and gather the family. As they rushed to his bedside, I looked down at my father and realized by the gray glaze over his eyes, that he had quietly slipped into a coma. For the next few moments, his beloved family stood by his bed and watched the now useless machines slowly register the life that was withdrawing from my father's still body. As the last level dropped to zero, my twin cried out, "Fight, Dad! Stay with us! Fight!"

I patted his lifeless hand and whispered, "Go to the light, Dad. It's all right. Go with Him to the light."

I could picture the Angel who awaited him at the foot of the bed, leading my father home.

*—Shirley Lakes*
*Shepherdsville, Kentucky*

God always has an angel of help for those who are willing to do their duty.

—T. L. Cuyler

# The Acts Angel

We loved our little conservative church. My husband was a respected deacon there and I headed up women's groups and Bible studies. We had been active in nearly every committee and had a hand in almost every stage of the church's growth over the years, making wonderful friends all along the way. If anyone would have told me that I was going to be torn away from my comfort zone there, I would have laughed at them.

One day, as I was making the bed, I collapsed onto it and found myself unable to move. I sensed that I wasn't alone, but the pressure over my body kept me from turning my head. I struggled against the force and eventually managed to position myself to see who was with me.

There in the corner was an Angel. It was huge, and was not contained by the room, its flowing mass went beyond the ceiling, floors, and walls.

In its hands were two flaming swords going back and forth. As they swung, the Angel spoke, saying over and over, "Acts 1:8, Acts 1:8, Acts 1:8 . . ."

I don't know how long the experience lasted but when the Angel vanished I got to my feet and scrambled for a Bible to find out what it said in Acts 1:8.

*"You shall receive power when the Holy Spirit has come upon you and you shall be witnesses to Me in Jerusalem . . . and to the end of the earth."*

I knew then and there that I needed to find a church where this scripture wasn't just read but was lived.

—*Ruth Busby*
*Goodletsville, Tennessee*

# Go Back

I was in an auto accident in 1980. I was driving home with my date when we were rear ended. Upon impact I was temporarily paralyzed and my back was broken to the point where two disks needed to be removed.

Before surgery, they administered a mylagram where they inject dye into the spine and create an image for the surgeon to study. For some reason though, I had a bad reaction to the chemicals they used which, I believe, caused me to die.

I watched from above as the medical team went into action, trying to resuscitate me. Nurses were slapping my face and hands, reporting to the doctor that my temperature was dropping.

I remember thinking that it was strange that I should be watching all of this, and wondered how it was possible that I could be airborne above them.

While in the air, an Angel came up beside me and in a soft voice said, "You must go back."

At the time I was a single mother raising two daughters alone. I thought of them as the voice spoke again, "Your job is not yet complete, you must go back."

A few hours later, I awoke.

My mom told me that the doctors nearly lost me. Had it not been for the advice of an Angel, they would have.

—*Judy G. Smith*
*Gladwin, Michigan*

# Hospital Visitor

I was in the hospital after being treated for my second heart attack. I was very depressed, feeling along and scared. I did not want to die, I had so many things I wanted to do.

I was confined to bed, sorting through my fears when a woman walked in. She was dressed in a hospital gown with a white satin robe over it, tied at the waist.

"I hear you are afraid of dying." she said.

I hadn't mentioned the internal struggle I was feeling with anyone.

"I just came by to tell you that you are going to be all right. You have not accomplished your purpose yet."

"I sure would like to know what that purpose is." I replied.

"It is something that is going to help a lot of people."

She paused, letting her words sink in and then said, "Everything will be okay."

I decided she must be a patient from a nearby room and asked my nurse about her. The nurse replied that nobody bearing my description was on the floor.

I did recover but wondered afterward just what my purpose was.

In 1995 my son died. After his death, I began writing a book about losing a child. I had to save my sanity and make his death count for something. I interviewed many others who have lost children and became a published author when it was all said and done.

My books have helped a lot of people make their way through the grieving process and I have counseled many moms who have lost their children as well, helping to bring hope where there had been a broken heart.

I remember the words of that Angel who came to my hospital room and foretold what was to come.

I know what my purpose is now, and will do what I was left here to do until she comes back to take me home.

*—Donna DeLaine*
*Ft. Myers, Florida*

Since God often sends us inspirations by means of His angels we should frequently return our aspirations to him by means of the same messengers.

—St. Francis de Sales

# My Angel Wings

My angel wings are brighter now,
They've turned to sparkling gold.
Because my parents gave to me
Their love that overflowed.
They taught me how to live in awe,
And view a clear blue sky.
Enjoy a crimson sunset,
Or a mountain way up high.
Because of them, I lived a life
Of wonder through and through.
So now my wings are golden bright
And shine soft rays on you.

—Andie Hellem

Make yourself familiar with the angels
and behold them frequently in spirit;
for without being seen,
they are present with you.

—St. Frances de Sales

# Backseat Angel

About two weeks ago, I prayed God would reveal Himself to me.

Not long after making that prayer, I was off to work on a Friday morning. I was cruising along at around 65 mph, when I was jolted from my thoughts by the sight of a 4 X 4 piece of lumber in the road. I swerved hard to miss it but nicked it just enough to see it fly up between a semi-truck and a van right behind me. I heard it hit my car but was glad to see I had made it through what could have been a real disaster.

# Angels Everywhere

As my rapid heartbeat began to slow down, the truck driver came up beside me, got my attention and let me know that I really needed to stop and take a look at the side of my car. As soon as I could, I pulled over to find the wooden post I nearly ran over had caused my rim to roll up away from the tire. Still, it had remained inflated. With just a few miles left to go, I went on in to work, dropping the car off at a nearby service station.

When I got there the garage owner said that in 50 years of service he had never seen tires stay up that were that badly damaged.

Minutes after pulling in. The tire blew.

I realized then that I had heard, loud and clear, an answer to my prayer. God was there, and that day, He had one of His Angels in my back seat.

—*V. Easely*
*Raleigh, North Carolina*
*Courtesy of He Invites,*
*Inc.*

# *My Sunday Angel*

used to go to work very early on Sunday mornings. During the winter months, it would still be quite dark when I arrived. The parking lot was never lit and usually empty when I got in. Even so, I always drove through it as if it were full of cars, taking the same route to my usual parking place.

One morning, I felt a certain lightness about me. It is difficult to explain but it made me want to get into my spot quicker than usual so I drove straight through the middle of the parking lot.

Later in the day, a customer came in and asked who he should notify about the hole in the parking lot. When I looked outside, I saw a four foot wide hole that was seven feet deep in the area I always drove through. It was definitely big enough to swallow my little compact car.

Looking back, only God knows how bad I would have been hurt, driving along and hitting the bottom of that sink hole. Thankfully though, that Sunday, buoyed by my Guardian Angel's lightness, I made it through okay.

*—Ms. Merrill Millwater*
*Glen Head, N.Y.*

# Everything Will Be Okay

In 1988, I was admitted to the hospital because I was terribly depressed. I had just found out my father had lung cancer and he had a one in five chance of making it another five years.

I was already taking prescribed medication for the anxiety I was fighting before all of this but once I was admitted it was taken from me.

One night, as I laid in bed, I was thinking about the mess I had made of my life. So much was going wrong. I was so sad.

## Angels Everywhere

All of a sudden, I heard a whisper in my ear. It was a male's voice that said, "Everything will be okay." I heard it loud and clear, and could almost feel the breath on my ear as he spoke. I was shocked, my eyes flew open and I looked around the room. There was no one there.

It never happened again but the voice was right. Bad things happen but I am okay thanks to some encouragement at the right moment from my unseen Angel.

*—Sharon LaCroix*
*Taunton, Massachusetts*

# Tea Stain Angel

Several weeks ago, after putting in a 17-hour day on my book, *Expect Miracles*, I went to get a cup of tea. It was very late as I shuffled into the kitchen.

Having done this many times in the past, I began pouring my tea but missed my mark and tea went everywhere.

Far too tired to clean it up, I took that as a sign that I should get some rest and went to bed.

The next morning, I woke up to an incredible sight. The tea I had spilled formed the shape of an Angel. Not only did it have shape but detail as well. She had a halo, wavy hair and a frilly skirt. In one hand she held a book and the other hand pointed to it.

I called my friend Ardy who was skeptical about it but came to take pictures of it for me anyway. Thinking it was only a coincidence, she went home convinced I was a little nuts.

When she got home, she lit a scented candle and went about her normal routine. Later, she came back to find it had melted everywhere. She let it cool and then began peeling up the wax. The biggest chunk she tossed over to the side thinking she'd put it in a drawer to make things smell pretty.

Later, her husband came in, picked up the chunk of wax and remarked, "Did you notice this looks just like an Angel?"

Amazingly, her wax Angel had delicate molded features with a perfect beautiful face.

What was even more remarkable was that our Angels were the same size. They both had wavy hair with frilly skirts and were nearly a match to each other in every detail.

# Tea Stain Angel

We don't question the existence of the angels around us, we just say "thank you" and keep looking for the next miracle. Sometimes they are small and hard to spot, but they are there for those who look for them.

> —*Mary Ellen*
> *Author of*
> Expect a Miracle
> *Conari Press, 1999*

If you seek an angel with an open heart...
you shall always find one.

—Anonymous

## Be Good and True

When I was a young girl, I woke up around 5 a.m. to find a figure standing at the foot of my bed. He was gold and orange, surrounded by a brilliant glow. It was much like the same kind of glow you'd see around clouds during a sunset.

As I looked at him, I was not afraid. Instead, I just stared at him, feeling safe and secure the whole time.

He began speaking to me and although I do not to this day remember what he said, I remember nodding, taking in everything he told me. I knew then he was my Guardian Angel.

# Angels Everywhere

I have been a full-time job for him ever since. I was in a head-on collision with a drunk driver going 70 mph. Even though I was not wearing a seatbelt (something everyone should do) I walked away with only bumps and bruises.

Another time, I was in a riding accident. The horse fell and all 700 pounds of him rolled over me. Again, I walked away with no injury.

I was even held up at gunpoint and still managed to avoid any harm. Throughout that and numerous other close calls, I have been convinced that my Guardian Angel was there, standing in the way of danger.

I have only seen him once since that appearance back in my youth. The night I met my husband-to-be, my golden Guardian Angel returned. This time, I heard him plainly and remember every word he spoke.

He told me, "Be good and true and you shall know love for the rest of your life."

His light and his warmth filled me with peace as it had done so long ago. "Every moment won't be glorious, but try to understand what your mate goes through and love him the way you know is true."

Then he vanished. His words though, have stayed with me ever since. My husband calls me HIS Angel now, and that is a nickname I will live by happily.

—*Kristi Heimrich*
*Las Vegas, Nevada*

Angels appreciate things about you that you thought no one else ever noticed.

—Anonymous

# What the Deaf One Heard

I have been deaf all of my life, but I tell you the truth when I say that I can hear the songs of Angels.

The first time I heard them, I was in the hospital. I was a small boy and had just gone through an operation in which doctors attempted to give me hearing. When the operation was over, the surgeon came into the room to explain to my parents that there was no way to correct this problem.

# Angels Everywhere

As he was talking to my Mom and Dad, I heard this wonderful noise. It was beautiful and comforting and warm. Then I began to see this light that came in flashes and sparkles, like the sun off of water, shimmering around the figures of Angles. They were invisible to everyone else, but I saw them clearly.

After that, I began to question whether they were really angels I saw that day, but years later at a friends' house, they returned to me. Although I verified with my friend that she couldn't hear a sound, I could hear them again. The light came back too and so did this mist that seemed to swirl and flow around them. I could see their robes, and a glow that outlined them. I go back there often now and enjoy being in their company.

The music they sing is unlike anything I can describe, but I can say that if you have not heard it, you have a treat waiting for you in heaven. It is clear and powerful and it stirs the soul.

I now know Angels are everywhere. They stand outside the door and sit beside you in the library. Sometimes they are someone you have just met and other times they walk right past you at a park sharing only a quick smile. Sometimes though, they are with me, singing a song that only the deaf one hears.

—*Bob Silverman*
*Winnetka, California*

An angel can illume the thought and mind of man by stretching the power of vision, and by bringing within his reach some truth which the angel himself contemplates.

—St. Thomas Aquinas

# The Blue-eyed Angel

**B**ack in 1997, I was a single girl, out of work and pregnant. I had considered giving my baby up for adoption and even had a nice couple picked out in New York who I thought would make great parents.

Once I decided to give the baby up though, I became quite depressed and found it difficult to function. I kept wrestling with my feelings and wondering about what really was best for me and my unborn child.

# Angels Everywhere

One dark and dismal day when I was vacuuming my trailer, I noticed a glow at the end of the hallway. The light got brighter with each second until it became almost blinding.

I walked into the light, squinting to see what the cause of this was. As I got closer, I saw a toddler with white curly hair and big blue eyes, sitting in the center of all that illumination. The baby wore a diaper so I couldn't tell whether it was a boy or a girl.

As my eyes filled with tears, the baby stretched out its arms and started to run toward me. I was so overwhelmed that I fell to the floor sobbing. When I looked up again, the light and the baby were gone.

I knew then that an Angel had given me this chance to see what I would be missing if I gave my child up. Right then and there I changed my mind, and on October 16, I gave birth to a baby boy with white curly hair and big blue eyes.

I'm so glad I kept him and I still cry when he reaches out to hug me.

—*Nichole Ohagan*
*Oklahoma City, Oklahoma*

# You Never Know

We were on our way to a Promise Keepers meeting 1,200 miles away, thinking we would turn this occasion into a family vacation while we were at it. Promise Keepers, for those who don't know, is an event where thousands of men gather in a stadium to pray and recommit themselves to God and to their families. It's a powerful time of fellowship with other Christian men that leaves nearly everyone who attends changed for the better.

# Angels Everywhere

My husband was eager to go and so we packed up the car and our three daughters and started for Maryland.

We had put over 800 miles behind us, and were marveling at how well the kids were behaving when our car broke down.

Here we were, hundreds of miles from home and hundreds of miles from our destination, sitting on the side of the road.

We called a tow truck and waited for help. As we sat there, we prayed for God to give us a hand.

The tow truck operator arrived, and we were happy to discover that he, too, was a Christian. We talked about church and Promise Keepers as we made the 40-mile trip to the service station.

Upon our arrival, the mechanic said it was a $60 repair. We were relieved because we figured we could afford that much . As we sat there and waiting, a man came in to have his car worked on as well.

His name was Dan and he was a nice man that seemed to warm up to my husband instantly. Like an old friend he listened to our plans and he seemed genuinly interested in how we were doing.

About then we got some bad news. The repairs would be $600. To make matters worse (and even more expensive) the mechanic would need another day to get the parts which would mean spending the night at a motel. This was far more than we could afford both financially and emotionally.

As my husband went outside to pray, Dan pulled out his credit card and paid the bill. When my husband discovered what had happened, tears filled his eyes as he shook Dan's hand. About then, a friend of Dan's named Russ arrive. He loaded us into a van and took us to a nearby hotel where again, the bill was paid.

I looked up at Russ and asked, "Have you ever seen that show 'Touched by an Angel'?"

He smiled, and said "Why do you ask?"

"I was just wondering if you were an Angel."

He grinned, winked and said, "You never know."

# Angels Everywhere

Dan smiled too and said, "You go ahead and enjoy the rest of your trip. Everything is going to be all right."

That night when we said our prayers, we thanked God for all He had done for us. You see, even though bad things were happening to us, God was right there making sure ALL our needs were met. It is so true, He NEVER does leave you nor forsake you. We are proof of that!

—*Denise Becker*
*Monticello, Minnesota*

# The Old Rabbi

In Maryland in 1974, my husband and I were in a small drugstore with our two young sons. We both noticed the loud coughing of an old man, who was bent and frail.

We looked at each other in concern — our youngest was very susceptible to respiratory illness and we both had the thought that he shouldn't be near this man.

The man came closer and despite my fears for my son, I wanted to ask him if he was all right.

# Angels Everywhere

He was well dressed and neat, with a coat appropriate for the cold evening but seemed lost and lonely.

I asked if he was okay. He said he needed to go back home and that he lived in a Hebrew home not far away. An employee of the store asked if he could make a phone call for him but the old man replied that it was so close that he would just walk there.

My husband and I agreed that he was to frail to walk even a few blocks in the bitter cold. So, in spite of our fear about exposing our boy to his hacking cough, we offered him a ride home. He accepted.

On the short ride, he spoke eloquently about our kindness. He said he was a rabbi and gave a blessing to each of our children. He was no longer so frail looking and seemed far from sick or senile. We were touched by his words and felt a thrill, like we were experiencing something extraordinary.

The rest of the way home, we talked about Angels, and both believed that we encountered one there, exchanging a simple act of kindness for a blessing.

# The Old Rabbi

Many times I have thought about the blessing bestowed on the boys by the rabbi that night. The words were, of course, in Hebrew, spoken in soothing song-like rhythm. He didn't say a lot but I still feel the strength of it.

There wasn't any dramatic change in the boys' health after the rabbi's blessing but I do remember feeling deeply concerned about their spiritual well-being. I was agnostic, very disenchanted with religion. I told myself that people had created God — that we used stories about God to smooth over all the rough, unfathomable things we couldn't understand. Religion was just a lullaby we used to soothe ourselves to sleep. I was never certain or happy with these conclusions, but content to drift along.

But my boys! Was it fair to raise them without any spiritual foundation? After meeting the rabbi, I couldn't rest on this issue.

I finally decided that it would be good to at least take them to church so they could learn the stories and they could make up their own minds someday.

# Angels Everywhere

It is hard to describe what it was like the first Sunday I walked into a church — announcing that I was just bringing them to Sunday school, and *yes* I guess I would sit in a class for the hour since I would have to wait somewhere.

Well, as you can guess, I went back (for the kids, of course,) over and over.

Eventually I recognized how God was pulling me back to him. I accept now that I will never understand God — religion will always be a mystery and my questions will remain unanswered in this life. There is no doubt though that God is real and powerful and that he loves each of us with an intensity and jealousy that we cannot begin to comprehend. My husband, amazed at the transformations in my attitude and at how happy I was, started coming to church. Soon he was baptized, too.

My little boys grew up learning about God's love and also chose to believe. A daughter came later — she too is a Christian, and now our youngest, David, has joined the ranks. He is so insightful about the things of God that our pastor believes he'll be a pastor, too, someday.

I'm grateful that God sent an Angel to spur me into thinking about giving my children a chance to know Him.

He could have sent a bolt of lightning.

*—Deborah Lane*
*Lexington, Kentucky*

# Special Thanks

In the course of researching this book, I came across a number of great web sites, and made some great friends along the way. I would like to gratefully acknowledge their help in getting this book prepared, and encourage you to visit them as well! You will be blessed!

Angels and Good News Letter
  www.angelscribe.com
Angel Truths: A Monthly Newsletter
  www.hometown.aol.com/rasprute
www.angelhaven.com
www.angelicexpressions.com
www.heinvites.org
www.bookdimensions.com
www.angelshop.com
www.intouchmag.com
www.angelfire.com/ma/myguardianangels
www.members.aol.com/hopefilled
www.tcastle.com
www.geocities.com/heartland/ranch9337

Please forgive me if I left anyone out and contact us at our website.

# Do You Have an Angel Story?

If you have a story you'd like to share with us,
come visit our web site at

## www.angelseverywhere.faithweb.com

or you can send us a letter at

**Angels Everywhere**
P.O. Box 857
White House TN 37188

We look forward to hearing your story!

## Premium gift books from PREMIUM PRESS AMERICA include:

I'LL BE DOGGONE
CATS OUT OF THE BAG

STOCK CAR TRIVIA
STOCK CAR GAMES
STOCK CAR DRIVERS & TRACKS
STOCK CAR LEGENDS

GREAT AMERICAN CIVIL WAR
GREAT AMERICAN COUNTRY MUSIC
GREAT AMERICAN GOLF
GREAT AMERICAN STOCK CAR RACING

ANGELS EVERYWHERE
MILLENNIUM MADNESS

ABSOLUTELY ALABAMA
AMAZING ARKANSAS
FABULOUS FLORIDA
GORGEOUS GEORGIA
SENSATIONAL SOUTH CAROLINA
TERRIFIC TENNESSEE
VINTAGE VIRGINIA

TITANIC TRIVIA
LEONARDO—TEEN IDOL

BILL DANCES FISHING TIPS
DREAM CATCHERS
THE REDNECK GUIDE TO WINE
   SNOBBERY

PREMIUM PRESS AMERICA  routinely updates existing titles and frequently adds new topics to its growing line of premium gift books. Books are distributed though gift and specialty shops, and bookstores nationwide. If, for any reason, books are not available in your area, please contact the local distributor listed above or contact the Publisher direct by calling 1-800-891-7323. To see our complete backlist and current books, you can visit our website at www.premiumpress.com.  Thank you.

**Great Reading.   Premium Gifts.**